animal attack!

WILD DOG ATTACKS

Suzanne J. Murdico

HIGH
interest
books

Children's Press
A Division of Grolier Publishing
New York / London / Hong Kong / Sydney
Danbury, Connecticut

For my father, Frank Eckert

Photo Credits: p. 5 © IndexStock; p. 6 © Ralph A. Clevenger/Corbis; p. 9 © St. Bartholomew's Hospital/Science Photo Library; pp. 11, 13 © Ralph Reinhold/Animals Animals; p. 12 © Charles Palek/Animals Animals; pp. 15, 33 © Paul A. Souders/Corbis; p. 17 © Carol Geake/Animals Animals; p. 18 © Zig Leszczynski/Animals Animals; p. 21 © Michael Maslan Historic Photographs/Corbis; p. 23 © Owen Franken/Corbis; pp. 24, 34 © Gerard Lacz/Animals Animals; p. 27 © 1994 NMSB/Custom Medical Stock Photography; p. 28 © Yann Arthus-Bertrand/Corbis; p. 30 © Des & Jen Bartlett/National Geographic Image Collection.

Visit Children's Press on the Internet at:
http://publishing.grolier.com

Library of Congress Cataloging-in-Publication Data

Murdico, Suzanne J.
  Wild dog attacks / by Suzanne J. Murdico.
    p.cm.—(Animal attack!)
  Includes bibliographical references.
  Summary: Explains why once-domesticated dogs become feral and band
    together in cities and looks at individual cases of feral dogs attacking
    humans.
  ISBN 0-516-23316-5 (lib. bdg.)—ISBN 0-516-23516-8 (pbk.)
   1. Feral dogs—Juvenile literature. 2. Animal attacks—Juvenile literature.
    [1. Feral dogs.
  2. Dogs. 3. Animal attacks.] I. Title.

SF810.7.D65 M87 2000
363.7'8—dc21
                                                    99-047511

contents

introduction

This book uses the term "wild dogs" to refer to household pets that have been left homeless by their owners. They have been abandoned. Some pets are abandoned because their owners no longer want them. Others are simply left alone to run loose for hours or even days at a time.

These wild dogs wander the streets looking for food and shelter. They often cause a lot of trouble. Without human care and training, these once lovable pets often become aggressive. They may attack people and other animals for no reason. When these wild dogs gang up in packs, they can become even more aggressive and dangerous to humans and other pets.

Wild dogs usually travel in groups.

Most stray dogs are not spayed or neutered. This means that they are able to have puppies. Wild dog packs often form around a female dog. These dog packs then have more puppies. These puppies grow up and also spend their lives on the street. The dog packs become larger and larger.

chapter one

MAN'S BEST FRIEND?

Edgar Alvarez, Jr., lives in Edmonton, Alberta, in Canada. One November morning, the six-year-old was coming out of his apartment on his way to the school bus. Just as he closed the apartment door behind him, four large Rottweiler dogs jumped on the small boy. Three of the dogs then began biting him. Ed Malinowski lives across the street from Edgar. Ed saw the attack from his window and ran out to help Edgar.

"Two dogs had him by each arm and the third one was pulling on his midsection," Malinowski told the Alberta Report *newspaper. "They were working*

A snarling Rottweiler

WILD DOG ATTACKS

together to tear him apart like he was a piece of meat. They were out for the kill."

Edgar's school bus had just pulled up. Anne Verhaeghe, the bus driver, saw the attack. The frightened children on the bus also watched the attack. Verhaeghe grabbed a broom and got off the bus. She heard Edgar screaming. Then suddenly the screaming stopped. "All I could hear was the dogs growling," she said. "I thought the dogs had killed him."

Verhaeghe ran toward the angry dogs and began hitting them with the broom. From inside the apartment, Edgar's father heard his son's screams. He opened the door and looked out into the yard. He quickly pried his son away from the dogs and pulled him inside the building.

Edgar survived the attack but had deep bites on his arm and leg. The dogs that attacked the young boy were owned by another neighbor who lived across the street. The animals had probably been trained as attack dogs. They had also probably been allowed to run loose.

The deep bites on this person's leg were caused by a dog attack.

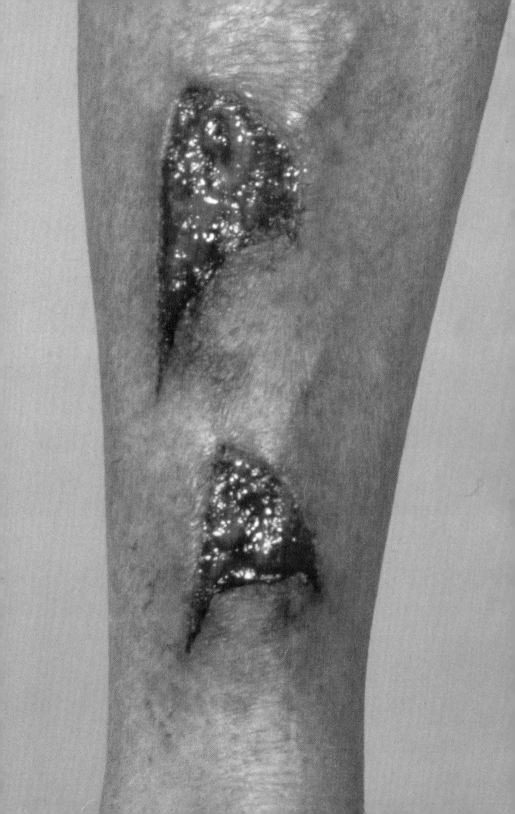

ATTACKS ON CHILDREN AND TEENS

The Humane Society of the United States says 60 percent of all dog-bite victims are children. This is because children are smaller in size and not as strong as adults. This makes children easier targets for dogs. Also, children like to play with dogs in a way that the dogs may see as threatening.

Jeff Chamblee, a fourteen-year-old from Texas, knows what it's like to be attacked by a pack of dogs. Laura Diane Mize was driving by the spot where Chamblee was attacked. She saw Chamblee on the ground. "He was lying flat on his back. The dogs were all around him, biting him," she reported in the *Amarillo Globe-News*.

When Mize reached Chamblee, the dogs ran off. The boy was covered in blood. Half of his clothes had been chewed off. The dogs came back, but Mize was able to keep them away. When other people came over to help, the dogs started attacking them, too. Chamblee was taken to the hospital

Most dogs are fun-loving pets.

to be treated for his injuries. A judge ordered that
the dogs be destroyed.

WHY DOGS ATTACK

What turns a family's pet into its worst enemy? Dogs
may attack people for many different reasons. Some

The police train German shepards to attack
violent suspects.

breeds are naturally more aggressive than others.
Many dogs have been trained to attack. Dogs may
bite or attack to defend the area in which they
live. This is called their territory. Dogs that don't
have much human contact may attack people, too.
This is because these dogs are not used to being
around people. They may think that people will try

to harm them. Dogs that have not been spayed or neutered are also more likely to attack.

Aggressive Breeds

Any type of dog might attack a person. However, some breeds are more likely to attack people than others. Some dogs are trained as attack dogs and may attack for no reason. They often attack when they are allowed to run loose. According to the Humane Society, two-thirds of deadly dog attacks are caused by five different breeds. These breeds are more likely than others to bite their victims more than once. Between 1979 and 1996, these dog breeds were responsible for the most deaths:

Pit bulls

Between 1979 and 1996, sixty people have died in attacks by pit bulls. Pit bulls are between 18 and 22 inches (45-55 cm) in height and

Pit Bull

weigh between 50 and 80 pounds (110-176 kg). Pit bulls are very strong. They have powerful muscles and strong jaws. When a pit bull bites, it's known to go for the throat. Once it grabs on, it hangs on until its jaws are pulled apart.

Rottweilers

Between 1979 and 1996, rottweilers have killed twenty-nine people during attacks on humans. Dogs in this breed range in height from 23 to 27 inches (57-67 cm) and weigh between 90 and 110 pounds (198-242 kg). They are muscular, power-ful, and are very protective of their territory.

German shepherds

Between 1979 and 1996, German shepards have killed nineteen people during attacks on humans. These dogs stand 23 to 25 inches (57-62 cm) tall and weigh between 75 and 95 pounds (165-209 kg). They are very intelligent animals and highly protective of their territory.

Huskies are known to be an aggressive breed of dog.

Huskies

Fourteen deaths happened between 1979 and 1996 because of huskie attacks. Most huskies are 20 to 24 inches (50-60 cm) tall. Their weight ranges from 35 to 60 pounds (77-132 kg). They are smart, quick, and athletic animals.

Alaskan malamutes

Twelve deaths happened between 1979 and 1996 because of Alaskan malamute attacks. These dogs are between 23 and 27 inches (57-67 cm) tall. They can weigh between 75 and 125 pounds (165-275 kg). They look similar to huskies but are larger and more powerful.

Defense of Territory

Dogs are territorial, which means that they have a certain area that is their own. For pet dogs, this area is their owner's home and yard. If a dog feels that its territory is threatened by a person, another dog, or another animal, the dog may attack. Have you ever

When behind a fence, a dog protects its territory by
snarling and barking at people passing by.

walked by a fenced yard where a dog behind the fence begins growling and barking at you? That dog is growling and barking at you in fear. You are close to its territory. It feels a need to defend itself by sending out a warning. The growling and barking are warnings for you to stay away.

Lack of Human Contact

Dogs that don't have much human contact are more likely to attack than others. This is because they are not loved, cared for, or trained by their owners. A dog that spends endless days chained up may become mean. Loneliness and lack of human care causes the animal to fear humans. Dogs react to fear by barking and growling. They even may attack.

This Doberman shows fear by defending itself. Often its defense turns into an attack.

chapter two

FROM PETS TO PREDATORS

Bucharest, the capital of Romania, is notorious for its wild dogs. More than 100,000 stray dogs roam the streets of this eastern European city looking for food and shelter. Each day, these dogs bite about fifty people.

The residents of Bucharest live in constant fear of being attacked by these dogs. "I was climbing the stairs to the Senate and a dog just jumped up and bit my leg," Irinel Radulescu told the Associated Press *news organization. Because of the dog bite, she needed to go to the hospital for shots.*

"And in the hospital courtyard, a dog almost bit me again," she said.

Wild dogs must always search for food.

WILD DOG ATTACKS

Even Hillary Rodham Clinton has been affected by Bucharest's wild dog problem. During the First Lady's visit to a hospital in the city, her security guards had to chase away a pack of wild dogs that were roaming around outside the building.

Why does Bucharest have more wild dogs than most other cities? Many people blame the problem on a former government leader, Nicolae Ceausescu. During the 1980s, Ceausescu ordered many homes torn down. In their place, he built government office buildings.

Because of these buildings, many people lost their homes. They had no choice but to move to apartments without yards. Although some dog owners were able to find new homes for their pets, others were not. Many people simply abandoned their dogs on the street. These stray dogs had no place to live. Hungry and thirsty, they roamed the streets in search of food and water. As they began to breed, the dog population problem increased.

Stray dogs have puppies that add to the huge dog population living on the streets.

In other areas with similar wild dog problems, the dogs are killed. Many people in Bucharest protested that plan. Instead, dog catchers catch as many dogs as possible. These dogs are taken to the dog pound. There, veterinarians give them a check-up and spay or neuter them. Then the dogs are returned to the streets. They still have no home.

WILD DOGS IN THE UNITED STATES

Bucharest is not the only city in the world in which wild dog attacks are common. In the United States, wild dogs can be found in cities and suburbs from coast to coast.

Wild Dogs in Detroit

In Detroit, Michigan, thousands of stray dogs wander the streets night and day. Although some of these dogs are alone, many others travel in packs of as many as twenty. Some wild dogs live in abandoned buildings throughout Detroit. Plans to demolish these buildings could create even more problems. Without these buildings that the dogs use, the wild dog population would be made to live on the city streets.

The wild dog problem was one of the top ten reasons for complaint from Detroit residents in 1998. Donyale Stephen, a city official, explains why. "A lot of people are saying that because of the

This samoyed has sharp teeth that can easily tear apart skin.

dogs, they're sometimes trapped in their homes," he told the Associated Press.

Detroit's wild dogs also scare postal workers. The Detroit postal workers must be on the lookout for wild dogs at all times. The wild dog problem is so bad that the city's postmaster has thought about stopping mail delivery in certain areas. "We've had carriers who have had [chunks of flesh] torn out of their arms and legs. There have been many postal workers who have had their clothes torn by dogs," explained Detroit mail carrier Johnnette Rule to the *Associated Press*.

Wild Dogs in Other Areas

Wild dogs have also attacked people in other parts of the United States. In Massachusetts, a young boy was attacked by a pack of wild dogs as he was walked to the bus stop. He escaped with just minor injuries. In Oklahoma City, wild dogs attacked several mail carriers.

Wild dogs also attack and kill animals. In

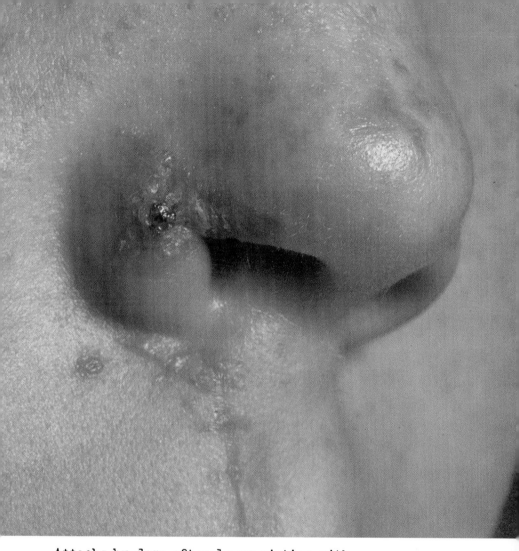

Attacks by dogs often leave victims with
lifelong scars.

Illinois, a pack of wild dogs killed more than
twenty-five pigs on a farm. These dogs could not
find food anywhere else, so they roamed through

a farm and found the pigs in their pens.

In Oregon, dogs killed two ostriches. In Tennessee, wild dogs killed a racehorse. In Colorado, dogs teamed up with coyotes—wild members of the dog family—to attack household pets and livestock (cattle and sheep).

JAPANESE FIGHTING DOGS

The Japanese fighting dog, called the Tosa, has been bred to be a fighter for hundreds of years. Today, Tosas are mostly bred as pets. You can see them in dog shows. However, illegal dog fighting still takes place in Japan. Tosas are bred by people to fight against each other. Sometimes these dogs fight until one has been killed by the other. This is inhumane treatment of animals. Worse, when these dogs can no longer make money for their owners, they are abandoned on the street. Bred for fighting, these street dogs are very dangerous to humans.

These Tosas are trained by their owners to fight.

chapter three

THE THRILL OF THE HUNT

The people living in Lagunitas, California, are keeping their pets inside their homes. A pack of four dogs has been attacking and killing wild animals. Homeowners are worried that their pets will be next. The wild dogs have killed two deer and a fox. They have also attacked a fawn. Although the dogs are probably someone's pets, they are allowed to run freely and cause problems.

Carol Gahagan, a Lagunitas resident, saw two of these wild dogs attack a deer. "There were dogs barking in a frenzy, as if they were on to something," she told the Point Reyes Light. *"Then I heard this awful groaning noise. I grabbed some*

Wild dogs often hunt in packs. These dogs have chased a lion up into a tree.

sticks and threw them at the dogs. Then I began screaming."

The dogs soon ran off, but not before seriously injuring the deer. They had bitten the deer's legs and throat. Although the wounded animal crawled away, it was not able to recover from its injuries. The Humane Society put it to sleep.

Wild dogs usually attack in pairs. That way, they can take on larger animals such as deer. And when they attack, they will fight for a long time before giving up.

"One of my neighbors literally saw a fox torn apart before his eyes by these dogs," Gahagan said. "They didn't stop, even when [my neighbor] sprayed them with a garden hose."

ATTACKS ON DOMESTIC ANIMALS

In Australia, large packs of wild dogs are hunting and killing livestock in rural areas of Queensland. Queensland is an Australian state. Some of these

Wild dogs often attack livestock, like these sheep.

packs contain one hundred or more dogs, including farm dogs, half-breeds, and dingoes. Dingoes are wild dogs commonly found throughout Australia. Few attacks on people have been reported. This

doesn't matter to the people who live there. Some residents of these areas are afraid to let their young children outside at night.

PREDATORY INSTINCTS

Domestic dogs are members of the *canidae* family of dogs. These also include such wild animals as wolves, coyotes, and foxes. Like their wild cousins, domestic dogs will learn how to fend for themselves if left on their own. Their natural survival instincts will help them find food to stay alive. In some cases, this means attacking and killing other animals for food. These animals are called prey. These wild dogs often work in packs so that they can help one another kill larger prey, such as deer and livestock.

Not all wild dogs attack for food, however. Many don't even eat what they kill. Some wild dogs simply get caught up in the thrill of the chase. If alone, one of these dogs probably would not attack. However, as part of a group, the dog is loyal to the pack and will follow the leader.

Dogs in packs show aggression toward each other, too.

THE FUTURE OF WILD DOGS
The future of wild dogs remains with dog owners around the world. The problem of abandoned pets must be solved first. This involves teaching responsible pet ownership.

Abandoned Pets
Why are dogs abandoned? Some people adopt a dog without realizing how much time, money, and patience is needed. Other people move to smaller homes where there's not enough room for pets. Sometimes those new homes have rules that do not allow pets. Still other people decide that they don't like or want the dog after they've taken it home.

Most people think that puppies are cute and loving animals. Often children talk their parents into buying them a puppy. When puppies are small and cute they get lots of attention. Owners are more likely to take better care of them. However, as puppies begin to grow and become more aggressive and need more attention, they must be trained. An untrained dog is an unmanageable animal. Training a dog properly takes time, energy, and dedication. Housebreaking a dog, teaching it to sit, to stay, not to jump on people, not to run away, and to behave, does not happen overnight. Often, training takes months before a dog becomes a good "family" dog. Unfortunately, many people find themselves owners of a dog much larger and more aggressive than they ever thought that cute puppy could grow into. Some owners try to find a new home for the dog. Others may simply leave the animal on the street. They hope that someone else will adopt the dog. That's not what usually happens.

did you know?

Dogs can't really "smell" fear. Fear has no real smell, like an orange does. But dogs can sense fear in people by how people move and react around them.

Instead, the dog becomes one more wild dog trying to survive on the street.

Responsible Pet Ownership

To reduce the number of dog attacks, dog owners must take care of their pets. "People need to realize that they are responsible for their animals and their animals need to be sterilized, socialized and trained," Janet Hornreich explained to the *Federal Times* newspaper. Hornreich works for the Humane Society of the United States.

Spaying and neutering dogs helps to avoid over-population and unwanted animals. Socializing dogs means making sure that they are used to being around people and will not feel threatened by them. Training dogs is important so that they will listen to their owner's commands. All of these activities help reduce the number of wild dogs and the number of dog attacks.

Responsible pet ownership also involves following leash laws. In many areas, leash laws require dog owners to keep their animals on a leash whenever the animal is in a public place. Leash laws help reduce the number of dog bites by making sure that dogs don't roam freely.

As pet owners become more aware of all dog-ownership issues, the wild dog problems around the world may decrease. However, people must begin to view dogs as more than just another "thing" to own. Dogs, when raised and treated with care and affection, are loyal and loving to their owners. They offer companionship and protection. For these reasons alone, they deserve our care and comfort.

FACT SHEET

Geographic Location

Like domestic dogs, wild dogs can be found throughout the world.

Life Span

ten to fifteen years

Number of Attacks on Humans

Each year, nearly one million people are treated for dog attacks. Millions of other attacks are not reported. *[Source: State Farm Insurance, May 1998]*

Between 1980 and 1996, dog attacks were responsible for 304 deaths. *[Source: Michigan Association of Insurance Agents]*

The wild dog heads on the map
show where wild dogs are found
throughout the world.

new words

abandon to give up responsibility for something, such as a job, a pet, or a child

aggressive showing mean behavior; ready to attack

breed type of animal; also, to produce offspring

domestic animal an animal that is tame

litter an animal's offspring

livestock farm animals, such as cattle and sheep, that are raised for food or profit

neuter to sterilize a male animal

predator an animal that hunts and kills other animals

prey an animal that is killed and eaten for food

spay to sterilize a female animal

sterilization a procedure that makes it impossible for an animal to produce offspring

territory an area that is occupied and defended by an animal or group of animals

for further reading

Hodge, Deborah. *Wild Dogs: Wolves, Coyotes and Foxes*. Toronto: Kids Can Press Ltd., 1997.

Ling, Mary. *Amazing Wolves, Dogs & Foxes*. New York: Alfred A. Knopf, 1991.

Murray, Kristy. *Man-Eaters and Blood-Suckers*. St. Leonards, Australia: Allen & Unwin, 1998.

Ryden, Hope. *Your Dog's Wild Cousins*. New York: Lodestar Books, 1994.

resources

American Society for Prevention of Cruelty to Animals (ASPCA)
424 E. 92nd St.
New York, NY 10128
www.aspca.org

Animal Protection Institute
2831 Fruitridge Rd.
Sacramento, CA 95820
www.api4animals.org

The Canadian Federation of Humane Societies
102-30 Concourse Gate
Nepean, Ontario, K2E 7V7
(888) 678-CFHS
www.cfhs.ca

Web Sites

Animal Attack Files

http://www.igorilla.com/gorilla/animal/

This site offers a great selection of news articles describing recent attacks on humans by animals. Included is a link to book lists for further reading.

Dog.com

http://www.dog.com

This site gives you facts about all breeds as well as health information for dogs. It also features dog-theme games and contests.

Electronic Zoo/NetVet: Dogs

http://netvet.wustl.edu/dogs.htm

This site offers dog breed information as well as information on other canines. It has many links to other dog-related Web sites.

Humane Society of the United States

http://www.hsus.org/

The Humane Society provides information on all of their issues and campaigns, as well as animal-related news and links to Animal Channel articles.

index

About the Author

Suzanne J. Murdico is a freelance writer who specializes in educational books. She has a degree in English and is the author of ten nonfiction books for children and teens. Suzanne has always loved animals. She did her college internship in the public relations department at the Philadelphia Zoo. Suzanne lives in New Jersey with her husband and their two tabby cats.